WALKWAYS OF THE PAST

Exploring the UK and Ireland's Forgotten Railways

Walkways of the Past: Exploring the UK and Ireland's Forgotten Railways Embark on a journey through time as Walkways of the Past takes you along the scenic remnants of once-thriving railway lines across the UK and Ireland. These abandoned tracks, now transformed into tranquil trails, are rich with history, natural beauty, and the echoes of industrial ingenuity.

From the breath taking estuaries of Wales' Mawddach Trail to the rugged Atlantic coastline of Ireland's Great Western Greenway, each chapter invites you to rediscover paths where steam trains once roared. Stroll along the idyllic Tarka Trail in Devon, cross the iconic viaducts of the Monsal Trail in Derbyshire, and wander the rolling landscapes of the Five Pits Trail. Every walk tells a unique story of resilience, renewal, and the enduring connection between communities and their landscapes.

Whether you're a history enthusiast, a nature lover, or simply seeking your next adventure, Walkways of the Past offers a vivid exploration of the hidden treasures that lie just beyond the horizon. Complete with detailed descriptions, fascinating historical anecdotes, and practical tips for every route, this book is your ultimate guide to uncovering the forgotten railways that shaped our world.
Step back in time. Rediscover the beauty of the journey. Walkways of the Past awaits.

Published 2018
Film Volt Group Publications
ISBN
978-1-326-78084-5

Chapter 1: The Camel Trail – Cornwall

"Where Tracks Once Rumbled, Nature Now Thrives"

Description of the Route

The Camel Trail meanders through one of Cornwall's most picturesque landscapes, offering 18 miles of flat, well-maintained paths ideal for walkers, cyclists, and families. Beginning in the quaint fishing town of Padstow, the trail follows the River Camel inland, passing through the lush greenery of the Camel Valley and ending in the historic town of Bodmin. An optional spur leads to the idyllic moorland of Wenford bridge.

This route is a blend of natural beauty and historical intrigue, allowing visitors to enjoy peaceful estuarine views, ancient woodlands, and remnants of railway heritage.

Historical Background

The Camel Trail occupies the former Bodmin & Wadebridge Railway, one of the oldest railways in the world. Established in 1834, it was initially designed to transport sand from the Camel Estuary to inland farms for use as fertilizer. Later, it also carried slate from the nearby quarries and, eventually, passengers eager to explore the Cornish countryside.

Key Historical Moments:

- **Early Days (1834–1840s):** One of the first railways in Cornwall, operated with horse-drawn wagons before transitioning to steam power.

- **Expansion (1870s):** Absorbed into the London & South Western Railway, the line became part of Cornwall's broader railway network.

- **Peak Usage (1920s):** The line thrived, particularly during the summer months, as visitors travelled to Padstow for seaside holidays.

- **Decline and Closure (1967):** Falling passenger numbers and the Beaching Axe led to its closure. By then, freight traffic had all but disappeared, and the railway's role in connecting rural communities waned.

- **Rebirth as a Trail (1980s):** Visionary conservationists transformed the abandoned railway into a recreational trail, preserving its legacy while inviting new generations to explore its path.

Closure and Transformation

The closure of the railway marked the end of an era for the communities it served. For a time, the tracks lay abandoned, overtaken by weeds and forgotten by most. But in the 1980s, local councils and nature organizations saw potential in the old railway. They cleared the tracks, repurposed bridges, and opened the trail to the public, creating what is now one of the UK's most beloved walking and cycling routes.

This transformation preserved the trail's industrial heritage while encouraging environmental conservation. Today, the Camel Trail is an essential part of Cornwall's tourism economy, drawing thousands of visitors annually.

Key Highlights Along the Route

1. Padstow Station:
The trail begins at the site of Padstow's old railway station, now a bustling harbour town famous for its seafood and picturesque views. Although the station itself has been repurposed, you can still find traces of its past in the surrounding area.

2. Camel Estuary:
The early part of the trail runs alongside the Camel Estuary, offering stunning views of tidal flats and salt marshes. This area is a haven for birdwatchers, with species like egrets, curlews, and oystercatchers commonly spotted.

3. Wadebridge:
Once a thriving market town, Wadebridge was a central hub for the railway. The old station platform remains visible, and the nearby bridge over the River Camel is a reminder of the town's historic importance.

4. Camel Valley Vineyards:
A short detour from the trail takes you to Cornwall's most celebrated vineyard, Camel Valley. Visitors can enjoy a wine tasting while taking in panoramic views of the surrounding countryside.

5. Bodmin:
The trail ends at Bodmin, a town steeped in history. The nearby Bodmin & Wenford Railway still operates as a heritage line, offering visitors a taste of steam train travel.

6. Wenfordbridge Spur:
For the more adventurous, the optional spur to Wenfordbridge takes you deeper into Cornwall's moorland. This remote section is quieter, with towering trees and ancient stone bridges adding to its charm.

Walkers' Experience
Walking the Camel Trail is a feast for the senses. In spring, the banks are adorned with wildflowers, and the air carries the scent of fresh grass and salt from the estuary. Summer brings longer days and an influx of activity, while autumn paints the trees in golden hues. Even in winter, the trail exudes a quiet beauty, with frost-covered branches and the misty river creating a dreamlike atmosphere.

The flat, even surface makes the trail accessible for all ages and abilities, and benches along the route provide ideal spots for rest or picnics. Families often enjoy the trail together, while solo walkers find it a tranquil escape.

Stories from the Trail

The Sand Trains:
In the early days of the railway, the sight of trains loaded with sand heading inland was a common sight. Farmers would eagerly await these deliveries, as the sand helped enrich Cornwall's acidic soil.

A Photographer's Paradise:
Local photographer Harriet Vivian famously captured images of the railway during its peak. Her photos, now preserved in local archives, provide a vivid glimpse into the trail's bustling past.

Memories of the Last Train:
When the railway closed, locals turned out in droves to bid farewell to the final passenger train. Many recall the bittersweet moment, as it marked the end of an era.

Practical Information for Walkers
- Length: 18 miles (shorter sections possible).

- Starting Point: Padstow, easily accessible by car or public transport.

- Difficulty: Easy; suitable for all levels.

- Best Time to Visit: Late spring to early autumn.

Nearby Attractions:
- The Eden Project, a short drive from Bodmin.

- Tintagel Castle, steeped in Arthurian legend.

- The Cornish coastline, with its golden beaches and dramatic cliffs.

Reflections on the Camel Trail

Walking the Camel Trail is more than a journey through Cornwall; it's a journey through time. Every mile reveals a story, from the hard-working sand trains of the 19th century to the vibrant recreation of today. As you follow the gentle curves of the trail, it's easy to imagine the hiss of steam engines and the chatter of passengers heading to seaside holidays.

The Camel Trail is a testament to the resilience of history, showing how forgotten railways can be transformed into something beautiful and enduring. Whether you're a railway enthusiast, a nature lover, or simply looking for a peaceful escape, this trail promises a memorable adventure.

Check out the local council website
https://www.cornwall.gov.uk/environment/countryside/cycle-routes-and-trails/the-camel-trail/

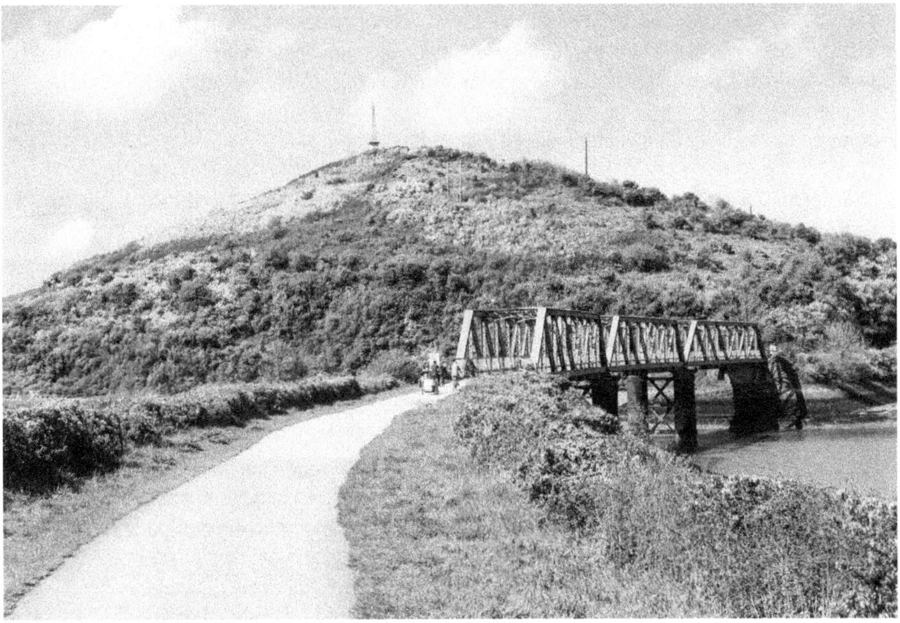

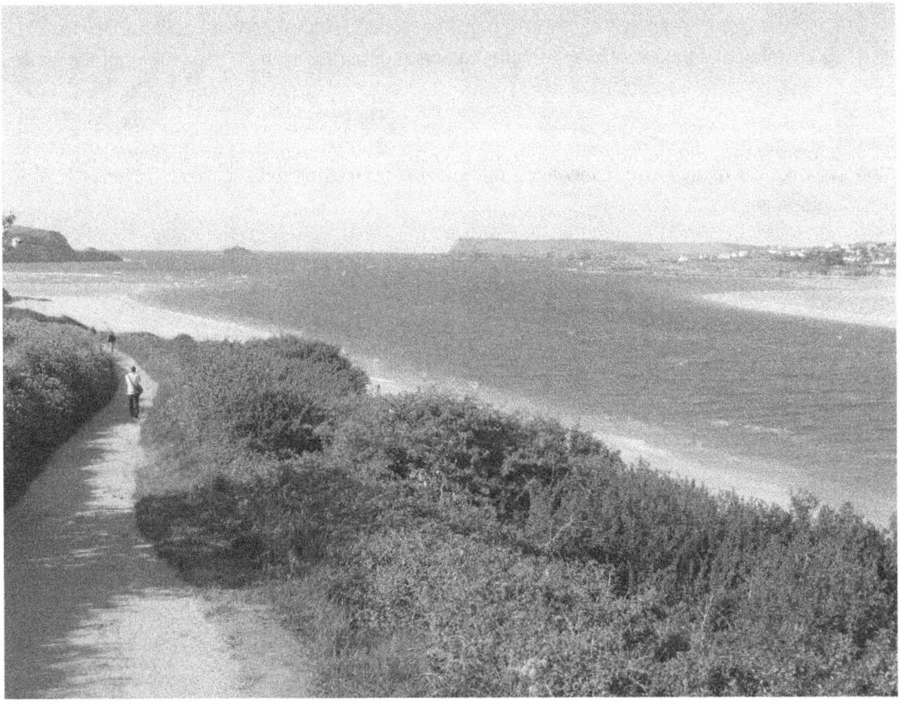

Chapter 2: The Monsal Trail – Derbyshire

"Where Engineering Meets Elegance in the Heart of the Peaks"

Description of the Route

The Monsal Trail stretches 8.5 miles through the heart of the Peak District National Park, following the route of the Midland Railway line that once connected Manchester to London. This picturesque trail combines stunning natural landscapes with remarkable feats of Victorian engineering. Starting in Bakewell, it meanders through valleys, over dramatic viaducts, and through lit tunnels, ending in the peaceful village of Blackwell Mill.

The Monsal Trail offers visitors an immersive experience in both history and nature, making it a favourite destination for walkers, cyclists, and history buffs alike.

Historical Background

The Midland Railway opened the line in 1863 as part of its effort to create a direct link between Manchester and London. At the time, the Peak District's rugged terrain presented a significant engineering challenge. Victorian ingenuity, however, triumphed, resulting in a railway that was both functional and visually striking.

For over a century, the line carried goods and passengers through the picturesque dales. It played a crucial role in connecting rural Derbyshire communities to larger urban centres, facilitating trade and tourism. However, the rise of road transport and the decline of rural rail services led to its closure in 1968 under the Beeching cuts.

Key Historical Moments

- The Rise of the Midland Railway (1860s): The Midland Railway constructed the line to establish dominance in railway transport, carving through the limestone valleys of the Peak District.

- Victorian Ingenuity: Engineers designed a series of tunnels, viaducts, and embankments to traverse the challenging landscape, with many of these features now listed as historical landmarks.

- Closure and Decline (1968): The closure marked the end of regular rail services in the region, leaving the route dormant for decades.

- Rebirth as the Monsal Trail (1981): Derbyshire County Council recognized the trail's potential as a recreational route, opening it to walkers and cyclists. The tunnels were initially closed but reopened in 2011 after restoration, making the entire route accessible once more.

Key Highlights Along the Route

1. Bakewell:
Famous for its namesake pudding, Bakewell serves as the starting point for the Monsal Trail. Though the old railway station has been repurposed, remnants of its past remain. Visitors often explore the town before embarking on the trail.

2. Headstone Viaduct:
Arguably the most iconic feature of the trail, this striking viaduct spans the River Wye near Monsal Head. Built in 1863, the viaduct offers breath taking views of the valley below. Initially criticized for its intrusion into the natural landscape, it is now celebrated as a harmonious blend of engineering and beauty.

3. Lit Tunnels:
The trail's four tunnels Headstone, Cressbrook, Litton, and Chee Tor—were essential for the railway to navigate the steep terrain. Restored and lit for public use, these tunnels offer a thrilling, atmospheric experience. The Headstone Tunnel, at 487 meters, is the longest and a favourite among visitors.

4. Water Cut Limestone Valleys:
The trail's path through the Wye Valley showcases dramatic limestone cliffs and clear river waters, creating a landscape that feels both tranquil and grand.

5. Millers Dale Station:
Once a bustling stop along the line, Millers Dale Station is now a heritage site. Visitors can explore its remaining platforms and learn about the station's role as a hub for local industries, including limestone quarrying.

6. Blackwell Mill:
The trail ends near Blackwell Mill, a peaceful hamlet that provides a sense of closure to the journey. Nearby is the stunning Chee Dale Nature Reserve, a haven for wildlife enthusiasts.

Closure and Transformation
The closure of the railway under the Beeching cuts devastated local communities, many of whom relied on the line for transport and commerce. For years, the abandoned tracks symbolized loss and neglect. However, the transformation into the Monsal Trail brought new life to the region. Restoration efforts included preserving key historical features, making the trail both a natural and cultural treasure.

Walkers' Experience
Walking the Monsal Trail is a sensory delight, with every step revealing a new perspective of the Peak District's beauty. The transition from open valleys to cool, echoing tunnels creates a dynamic experience, while the occasional relic of railway infrastructure sparks curiosity about the past.

The flat, well-maintained path makes the trail accessible to walkers of all levels. Cyclists also frequent the route, and benches along the way provide ideal spots for resting and taking in the views. Spring brings wildflowers along the banks, while autumn paints the valleys in hues of gold and crimson.

Stories from the Trail

"A Viaduct Too Beautiful to Hate"
When the Headstone Viaduct was completed, critics decried it as an eyesore that marred the pristine valley. Poet John Ruskin famously condemned it, writing:

"The valley is gone, and the Gods with it."
Over time, however, locals and visitors grew to appreciate the viaduct's elegant arches, and it is now one of the most photographed landmarks in the Peak District.

"The Final Train Journey"
In 1968, hundreds gathered to witness the last train pass through the route. For many, it was a bittersweet moment, marking the end of an era. Stories from that day recount the emotional farewells of railway workers and passengers who had relied on the line for decades.

"Rediscovering the Tunnels"
When the tunnels reopened in 2011, local residents shared tales of childhood adventures exploring the abandoned passages. Many remarked on how the reopening connected communities once again, this time through tourism and recreation.

Practical Information for Walkers
- Length: 8.5 miles (linear).

- Starting Point: Bakewell or Blackwell Mill, with parking and facilities available at both ends.

- Difficulty: Easy; suitable for all ages and abilities.

- Best Time to Visit: Spring and autumn, when the weather is mild, and the landscape is at its most vibrant.

Nearby Attractions:
- Chatsworth House, an iconic stately home located near Bakewell.

- The village of Monsal Head, offering panoramic views and cozy pubs.

- The Blue John Caverns, a short drive from the trail.

Reflections on the Monsal Trail
Walking the Monsal Trail is a journey that bridges past and present. The marvels of Victorian engineering, from its graceful viaducts to its atmospheric tunnels, stand as reminders of a time when railways represented the height of innovation. Today, these features coexist with the natural beauty of the Peak District, creating a trail that is as educational as it is enjoyable.

Whether you're drawn by history, scenery, or the sheer joy of walking, the Monsal Trail offers an experience that lingers long after you've left its path.

Chapter 3: The Strawberry Line – Somerset

"Tracing the Sweet Journey of Somerset's Strawberries"

Description of the Route

The Strawberry Line is a 10-mile pathway steeped in both natural beauty and local history. This flat and accessible route stretches from the village of Yatton to the dramatic cliffs of Cheddar, passing through a patchwork of orchards, woodlands, and rolling Somerset countryside. The name "Strawberry Line" harkens back to its days as a key transport route for locally grown strawberries, linking the Cheddar Valley's rich agricultural produce with broader markets.

Today, the trail offers a serene escape for walkers, cyclists, and families, winding through quiet villages and along the foot of the Mendip Hills.

Historical Background

The Strawberry Line was part of the Cheddar Valley Railway, a branch of the Great Western Railway. Opened in 1869, it primarily served as a freight line, transporting goods, coal, and the region's famous strawberries to markets in Bristol and beyond. Passenger services soon followed, and the line became an important link for rural communities.

Key Historical Moments:

- **Initial Construction (1869):** Built to connect Yatton with the Cheddar Valley, the railway rapidly became integral to local commerce.

- **The Strawberry Boom (1890s):** The line gained its nickname as demand for Cheddar Valley strawberries soared, particularly in London.

- **War and Change (1940s):** During WWII, the railway played a crucial role in transporting war materials.

- **Decline and Closure (1963):** The rise of road transport and the Beeching cuts led to the line's closure. Its tracks were dismantled, but its legacy endured.

- **Rebirth as a Trail (1980s):** Local conservation groups transformed the abandoned railway into a public walkway, preserving its memory and providing a space for leisure and nature appreciation.

Closure and Transformation

The closure of the Strawberry Line in 1963 marked a turning point for the Cheddar Valley. While the railway's closure disrupted rural connectivity, it also spurred a movement to preserve the line's cultural and natural heritage. Local volunteers and councils collaborated to repurpose the route as a multi-use trail, emphasizing its environmental and historical significance.

Today, the Strawberry Line is not just a walking path; it's a living museum of Somerset's past, blending industrial relics with vibrant ecosystems.

Key Highlights Along the Route

1. Yatton Station:
The trail begins at Yatton, where the old Victorian station still stands. This charming structure retains much of its original character and serves as a poignant reminder of the railway's heyday.

2. Strawberry Orchards:
As the trail heads out of Yatton, it passes through areas that were once covered in strawberry fields. Today, the remnants of these orchards can still be seen, and in summer, the air is sweet with the scent of fruit.

3. Congresbury Viaduct:
This impressive brick viaduct, spanning the River Yeo, is a testament to Victorian engineering. Standing beneath its towering arches, it's easy to imagine the sound of steam engines chugging overhead.

4. The Shute Shelve Tunnel:
One of the most atmospheric sections of the trail, the Shute Shelve Tunnel is a 165-meter-long passage through the Mendip Hills. Cool and dark, it provides a thrilling change of scenery. Its walls bear the marks of its construction, offering a tactile connection to the past.

5. Cheddar Reservoir:
A detour near Axbridge leads to Cheddar Reservoir, a tranquil spot for birdwatching and picnics. The reservoir's still waters reflect the surrounding hills, creating a picture-perfect scene.

6. Cheddar Village:
The trail concludes in Cheddar, home to the famous Cheddar Gorge and caves. Visitors can explore the village's historic streets, sample local cheese, or hike the nearby cliffs for breath taking views.

Walkers' Experience
Walking the Strawberry Line is a gentle yet rewarding journey. The flat path makes it accessible to people of all ages and fitness levels, and the trail is dotted with benches and picnic spots. Each season offers a different perspective:

- **Spring**: Wildflowers carpet the trail's edges, and birdsong fills the air.

- **Summer:** The lush greenery and occasional berry bushes evoke memories of the railway's agricultural heritage.

- **Autumn:** Golden leaves blanket the path, and the scent of ripening apples wafts from nearby orchards.

- **Winter:** Frost clings to the hedgerows, and the trail offers a peaceful retreat from the hustle of modern life.

The route is particularly popular with families and dog walkers, and its proximity to villages means there are plenty of opportunities to stop for refreshments along the way.

Stories from the Trail

"The Strawberry Express"
In the late 19th century, the Cheddar Valley Railway was inundated with crates of strawberries during harvest season. Trains carrying this precious cargo were nicknamed the "Strawberry Express." Local children would often sneak tastes of the fruit, plucking a few berries from the loaded wagons as they passed.

"A Line of Escape"
During WWII, the railway served not only as a supply line but also as an evacuation route for children fleeing urban bombing raids. Families from Bristol often sent their children to the safety of Somerset via the Strawberry Line, making it a lifeline during troubled times.

"Tunnel Tales"
The Shute Shelve Tunnel is the subject of many local legends. Some say the tunnel is haunted by the ghost of a railway worker who died during its construction. Walkers have reported hearing faint whispers or the echo of phantom footsteps within its dark confines.

Practical Information for Walkers
- Length: 10 miles (linear).
- Starting Point: Yatton Station, with ample parking and nearby public transport.
- Difficulty: Easy; suitable for walkers, cyclists, and families.
- Best Time to Visit: Spring and summer for the best weather and most vibrant scenery.

Nearby Attractions:
- The village of Axbridge, with its medieval square and museum.
- Cheddar Gorge, a natural wonder and popular hiking destination.
- The Mendip Hills Area of Outstanding Natural Beauty, perfect for exploring beyond the trail.

Reflections on the Strawberry Line

The Strawberry Line offers a unique combination of history, nature, and nostalgia. As you walk the path, you can almost hear the rumble of trains and smell the fresh strawberries that once defined this route. The trail is more than a walkit's a celebration of Somerset's heritage, a reminder of the region's resilience, and a testament to the community's commitment to preserving its past.

Whether you're a history enthusiast, a nature lover, or simply looking for a scenic escape, the Strawberry Line promises a journey as sweet as its name.

Chapter 4: The Cinder Track – North Yorkshire

"A Coastal Journey Through Time"

Description of the Route

The Cinder Track runs for 21 miles along the North Yorkshire coast, following the route of the former Whitby, Redcar, and Middlesbrough Union Railway. Stretching from the bustling seaside town of Scarborough to the historic fishing village of Whitby, the trail combines dramatic coastal views with a glimpse into the region's industrial heritage.

Named after the cinders once used to surface the railway bed, the track is now a popular destination for walkers, cyclists, and nature lovers. Its route offers a mix of rugged cliffs, serene woodlands, and charming villages, with the sea as a constant companion.

Historical Background

The Whitby, Redcar, and Middlesbrough Union Railway opened in 1885 as part of an ambitious plan to connect coastal communities and boost the local economy. The line primarily carried freight, including Whitby jet, alum, and ironstone, but also became a vital transport link for passengers traveling to seaside resorts.

At its peak, the railway provided an essential connection between the North Yorkshire coast and the industrial hubs of the northeast. However, as road transport gained popularity, passenger numbers declined, and the line eventually closed in 1965 following the Beeching cuts.

Key Historical Moments:

- **Construction (1880s):** Engineers faced significant challenges building the railway, particularly along the steep coastal cliffs and rugged terrain.

- **Economic Impact (1900s):** The line supported local industries, such as alum mining and the jet trade, while boosting tourism in Whitby and Scarborough.

- **Closure and Decline (1965):** The railway's closure marked the end of an era for the communities it served.

- **Rebirth as a Trail (1980s):** Local initiatives repurposed the track as a multi-use path, preserving its route for public enjoyment.

Closure and Transformation

When the railway closed, the track bed was left abandoned for years, overgrown and forgotten by many. In the 1980s, local councils and conservation groups recognized the route's potential as a recreational trail. By clearing the cinder-surfaced path and reinforcing its historic bridges, they transformed the track into a haven for walkers and cyclists.

The track's rugged surface retains its industrial character, and its meandering route offers visitors an opportunity to connect with both nature and history.

Key Highlights Along the Route

1. Scarborough Station:
The trail begins at Scarborough Station, a grand Victorian structure that remains a hub for train travel today. The station is a fitting starting point, reminding visitors of the railway's pivotal role in the town's development as a seaside resort.

2. Cloughton Woods:
A short distance from Scarborough, the track enters Cloughton Woods, a tranquil section filled with birdsong and dappled light. This area is perfect for a quiet stroll or a picnic.

3. Robin Hood's Bay:
This charming fishing village is a highlight of the route, with its narrow cobbled streets and picturesque cottages. The village's history as a smuggling hotspot adds intrigue to its already enchanting character.

4. Whitby Abbey:
Perched high on the cliffs above Whitby, the ruins of Whitby Abbey are visible from the trail. The abbey, famously associated with Bram Stoker's Dracula, offers breathtaking views of the town and the North Sea.

5. Viaducts and Bridges:
The track features several impressive viaducts, including the Larpool Viaduct near Whitby. This red-brick structure spans the River Esk and is a stunning example of Victorian railway engineering.

6. Coastal Views:
Throughout the route, the North Sea's dramatic vistas are a constant presence. The cliffs, beaches, and crashing waves create an ever-changing backdrop for walkers.

Walkers' Experience
Walking the Cinder Track is a sensory adventure. The salty tang of the sea breeze mingles with the earthy aroma of woodlands, while the sound of waves contrasts with the crunch of cinders underfoot. The route is moderately challenging, with a few inclines, but its rewards are plentiful.

Each section of the trail offers a different experience:

- From Scarborough to Ravenscar: This stretch features rolling fields and sweeping coastal views. Ravenscar, known as "the town that never was," provides an interesting historical detour.

- From Ravenscar to Robin Hood's Bay: A highlight of the trail, this section includes dramatic cliff-top walks and the chance to explore the village's smuggling past.

- From Robin Hood's Bay to Whitby: The final leg takes walkers through lush greenery and past the imposing Larpool Viaduct, culminating in the historic town of Whitby.

Stories from the Trail
"The Jet Line"
In the late 19th century, Whitby jet was in high demand for its use in Victorian mourning jewelry. The railway played a vital role in transporting this precious material from the mines to markets across the UK. Stories from the time describe how miners would load crates of jet onto waiting trains, which sped them to distant cities.

"Ravenscar: The Town That Never Was"
Planners once envisioned Ravenscar as a bustling seaside resort to rival Scarborough. The railway was built with this ambition in mind, but the rugged terrain and lack of natural beaches doomed the project. Today, remnants of this failed dream can still be seen in the village.

"The Ghost Train of Whitby"
Legend has it that on misty nights, the sound of a phantom train can still be heard near the Larpool Viaduct. Local folklore attributes this to the spirits of workers who died during the railway's construction, forever tied to the line.

Practical Information for Walkers
- Length: 21 miles (linear).
- Starting Point: Scarborough Station; ample parking and facilities available.
- Difficulty: Moderate, with some inclines and uneven surfaces.
- Best Time to Visit: Summer for clear coastal views, or autumn for the striking colours of the surrounding countryside.

Nearby Attractions:
- Scarborough Castle, overlooking the sea.
- The Whitby Museum, which features exhibits on local history and the jet trade.
- Sandsend Beach, a peaceful spot just outside Whitby.

Reflections on the Cinder Track
The Cinder Track is more than a walking route; it's a journey through North Yorkshire's industrial and cultural heritage. Every step tells a story, from the thriving jet trade of the 19th century to the quiet villages that endured the railway's closure. The trail's blend of history and natural beauty makes it a must-visit for anyone seeking a deeper connection to the region.

Walking the Cinder Track is a reminder of how landscapes evolve, where nature reclaims what industry left behind. It's a trail of contrasts past and present, wilderness and civilization, sea and land all woven together in a timeless tapestry.

Chapter 5: The Deeside Way – Aberdeenshire, Scotland

"From Granite City to Royal Retreat"

Description of the Route

The Deeside Way is a 41-mile trail running from the bustling city of Aberdeen to the tranquil village of Ballater in the Cairngorms National Park. Following the route of the former Royal Deeside Railway, the trail takes walkers through some of Scotland's most breath taking landscapes. Along the way, it passes through charming villages, ancient woodlands, and rolling countryside, all against the dramatic backdrop of the River Dee.

Known for its royal connections this railway once carried Queen Victoria and the royal family to Balmoral Castle the Deeside Way is steeped in history, offering visitors a chance to walk in regal footsteps while enjoying the natural beauty of Aberdeenshire.

Historical Background

The Royal Deeside Railway opened in 1853 as a crucial transport link between Aberdeen and the remote communities of Royal Deeside. It quickly became famous for its royal connections, with Queen Victoria and Prince Albert frequently using the line to travel to their beloved Balmoral Castle. The railway facilitated trade, tourism, and communication in the region, cementing its place in the social and economic fabric of Aberdeenshire.

Key Historical Moments:

- **Opening of the Line (1853):** The Deeside Railway was celebrated for connecting rural communities to Aberdeen, the "Granite City."

- **Royal Patronage (1850s–1900s):** The line gained international fame as Queen Victoria's preferred route to Balmoral. A special royal carriage was commissioned to ensure comfort and privacy for the royal family.

- **Decline and Closure (1966):** Like many rural railways, the line succumbed to the Beeching cuts, leaving a void in local transportation.

- **Rebirth as a Trail (2000s):** The abandoned railway was transformed into the Deeside Way, preserving its legacy and creating a vital recreational space.

Closure and Transformation

The closure of the Royal Deeside Railway marked the end of an era for the region. Communities that had relied on the railway for decades faced challenges as road transport became the primary means of travel. However, in the early 2000s, local councils and conservation groups worked to repurpose the railway route as a walking and cycling trail. This transformation not only preserved the path's history but also created a vital link for outdoor enthusiasts and nature lovers.

Today, the Deeside Way stands as a symbol of renewal, blending Aberdeenshire's cultural heritage with its stunning natural environment.

Key Highlights Along the Route

1. Aberdeen:
The trail begins in the vibrant city of Aberdeen, known as the "Granite City" for its striking grey-stone architecture. The old Aberdeen Joint Station, now modernized, hints at the city's railway past.

2. Cults and Biel side:
These affluent suburbs of Aberdeen offer a gentle introduction to the trail. Passing through tree-lined streets and well-kept parks, this section of the Deeside Way provides a peaceful transition from city to countryside.

3. Drumoak:
A small village with significant history, Drumoak is home to the ruins of Drum Castle, one of Scotland's oldest tower houses. The castle's history dates back to the 13th century, adding a medieval charm to the journey.

4. Crathes Castle:
This iconic castle, set amid beautifully landscaped gardens, is a highlight of the trail. Visitors can explore the castle's interior or wander through its enchanting grounds. Crathes is also a perfect spot for a picnic.

5. Banchory:
Known as the "Gateway to Royal Deeside," Banchory is a lively market town with a strong connection to the railway's history. The old station building has been repurposed as a community hub, and the River Dee here is popular for fishing and kayaking.

6. Aboyne:
As the trail progresses into more rural territory, Aboyne offers a tranquil setting with expansive views of the Cairngorms. The village's Victorian charm remains intact, with several preserved railway artifacts.

7. Ballater:
The trail concludes in Ballater, a picturesque village often associated with the royal family. The old Ballater Station, destroyed by fire in 2015 and rebuilt as a visitor center, once served as the royal family's stop for Balmoral Castle. The station's elegant design reflects its regal history.

8. Balmoral Castle (Optional Detour):
Although not directly on the trail, Balmoral Castle is a short distance from Ballater. A visit to this royal residence provides a deeper connection to the trail's history.

Walkers' Experience

Walking the Deeside Way is an unforgettable journey through Scotland's varied landscapes. The trail transitions from urban areas to lush woodlands, riverbanks, and open moorlands. The River Dee is a constant companion, its crystal-clear waters and occasional sightings of salmon adding to the experience.

- **Wildlife:** The Deeside Way is a haven for wildlife enthusiasts, with opportunities to spot red squirrels, deer, otters, and a wide variety of birds, including ospreys and golden eagles.
- **Seasonal Beauty:**
  - **Spring:** Blossoming trees and wildflowers along the trail.
  - **Summer:** Warm days perfect for picnics and exploring villages.
  - **Autumn:** Golden hues and crisp air make the trail particularly enchanting.
  - **Winter:** Frosty landscapes and the chance of snow transform the route into a winter wonderland.

Stories from the Trail
"The Royal Train"

Queen Victoria's journeys on the Royal Deeside Railway were legendary. Her diaries often mention her love for the scenic route, describing the river's beauty and the surrounding hills. Locals would gather at stations to catch a glimpse of the royal train, a source of pride for the community.

"The Deeside Express"

The line was not just for royalty. In its heyday, the Deeside Express was a popular service that connected rural Aberdeenshire with the bustling city of Aberdeen. It carried everything from farm produce to letters and livestock, forming a lifeline for isolated communities.

"The Haunted Viaduct"

Local legend tells of a ghostly figure seen walking the Cambus O'May viaduct near Ballater. Thought to be the spirit of a railway worker who died during its construction, the apparition is said to appear on misty nights.

Practical Information for Walkers
- Length: 41 miles (linear).
- Starting Point: Aberdeen; accessible by train and road.
- Difficulty: Moderate, with some uneven sections and gentle inclines.
- Best Time to Visit: May through September for the best weather and most vibrant scenery.

Nearby Attractions:
- Drum Castle and Crathes Castle, both rich in history and surrounded by stunning gardens.
- The Cairngorms National Park, perfect for further exploration.
- Royal Lochnagar Distillery, near Balmoral, for a taste of Scotland's famous whisky.

Reflections on the Deeside Way

The Deeside Way offers a unique blend of royal history, natural beauty, and community heritage. From the grandeur of Balmoral Castle to the simple charm of village life, this trail invites walkers to explore Aberdeenshire at their own pace. It is a journey through time and a celebration of the enduring legacy of the Royal Deeside Railway.

For those who take the path, the Deeside Way promises more than a walk—it promises a connection to Scotland's rich past and a profound appreciation for its timeless landscapes.

Chapter 6: The South Tyne Trail – Cumbria

"Climbing to England's Highest Narrow-Gauge Railway"

Description of the Route

The South Tyne Trail stretches for 23 miles through the dramatic landscapes of the North Pennines, following the path of the former Haltwhistle to Alston branch line. It is one of England's most scenic rail-to-trail routes, weaving through lush valleys, rolling hills, and rugged moorlands. Starting in the town of Haltwhistle, the trail climbs steadily to Alston, the highest market town in England, and concludes in the quiet hamlet of Slaggyford.

The trail is celebrated for its peaceful remoteness, iconic stone viaducts, and the historical charm of the South Tynedale Railway, a preserved narrow-gauge heritage line that operates part of the route.

Historical Background

The South Tyne Trail owes its origins to the Haltwhistle to Alston branch line, which opened in 1852. Known for being the highest narrow-gauge railway in England, the line was constructed to transport lead, coal, and other minerals from the surrounding Pennines. Over time, it became a vital passenger service, connecting rural communities to larger markets and towns.

Despite its success in earlier years, the rise of road transport and declining demand for mineral freight led to the railway's closure in 1976. Today, the route has been reborn as a popular walking and cycling trail, blending industrial heritage with the natural splendour of the North Pennines.

Key Historical Moments:

- **Opening of the Line (1852):** The railway opened to great local excitement, providing a lifeline for isolated communities in the Pennines.

- **Expansion of Services (19th Century):** Passenger services flourished, and the railway became a crucial link between Alston and Haltwhistle.

- **Economic Decline (1940s–1970s):** The collapse of the lead and coal industries, coupled with increased competition from road transport, spelled the end for the railway.

- **Closure (1976):** The line's closure marked the end of regular train services to Alston.

- **Heritage Revival (1983):** The South Tynedale Railway Society was formed to preserve a section of the line, reopening it as a narrow-gauge heritage railway.

Closure and Transformation

The closure of the Haltwhistle to Alston line in 1976 was a significant loss for the communities it served. For years, the abandoned tracks lay dormant, but local efforts to preserve the railway's legacy eventually led to its rebirth. The South Tyne Trail was officially established in the 1980s, creating a multi-use path that attracts walkers, cyclists, and railway enthusiasts.

The South Tynedale Railway, a volunteer-run heritage line, now operates a portion of the original route. Visitors can ride restored narrow-gauge trains through the scenic South Tyne Valley, experiencing the railway as it once was.

Key Highlights Along the Route

1. Haltwhistle:
Known as the "Centre of Britain" due to its location near the geographic midpoint of the UK, Haltwhistle is a charming market town and the starting point for the trail. The town's railway station still operates as part of the Tyne Valley Line, linking the area to Newcastle and Carlisle.

2. Featherstone Castle:
A short detour from the trail leads to this picturesque, privately owned castle. Its medieval origins and riverside setting make it a favourite spot for photographers and history buffs.

3. Lambley Viaduct:
One of the most iconic features of the trail, the Lambley Viaduct is an architectural marvel. This 260-meter-long stone structure spans the South Tyne River, offering stunning views of the valley below. Restored for pedestrian use, it's a must-see highlight.

4. Slaggyford Station:
This preserved station is a key stop for the South Tynedale Railway. Visitors can explore the station's history and catch a heritage train to Alston.

5. Alston:
England's highest market town is rich in history and charm. With its cobbled streets, historic buildings, and friendly atmosphere, Alston provides a rewarding endpoint for the trail. The South Tynedale Railway headquarters and the nearby Nenthead Mines Heritage Centre are key attractions.

6. Moorland Landscapes:
As the trail ascends into the North Pennines, walkers are treated to expansive views of heather-covered moors, crisscrossed by stone walls and dotted with grazing sheep.

Walkers' Experience
Walking the South Tyne Trail is a journey through solitude and serenity. The trail's gradual incline, from the lowlands near Haltwhistle to the high moors around Alston, offers a variety of terrains and ecosystems. The route is well-marked and maintained, making it accessible for walkers of moderate ability.

Seasonal Beauty:
- **Spring:** Bright wildflowers bloom along the path, and lambs frolic in the fields.
- **Summer:** Warm days reveal the vibrant greens of the valleys and the purple haze of flowering heather.
- **Autumn:** Golden hues and crisp air create an inviting atmosphere.
- **Winter:** Snow transforms the Pennines into a magical landscape, though walkers should prepare for icy conditions.

Stories from the Trail

"The Workers' Viaduct"
The construction of Lambley Viaduct was a monumental task in the 19th century. Local laborers, known as navvies, worked in harsh conditions to build the 9-arch structure. Today, their efforts stand as a testament to Victorian engineering and determination.

"The Final Train"
When the last train ran in 1976, hundreds of residents gathered to bid farewell. The event was both celebratory and bittersweet, marking the end of an era. Many passengers carried tokens of the journey, from tickets to coal, as keepsakes of the railway they loved.

"Legends of the Moor"
The moorlands around Alston are steeped in folklore. One tale speaks of a ghostly figure who appears on foggy nights near Lambley Viaduct, said to be the spirit of a railway worker who died during its construction.

Practical Information for Walkers
Length: 23 miles (linear).
Starting Point: Haltwhistle, with parking and public transport links.
Difficulty: Moderate; a steady incline with some uneven terrain.
Best Time to Visit: Spring and summer for mild weather and blooming landscapes.

Nearby Attractions:
Hadrian's Wall, a UNESCO World Heritage site located near Haltwhistle.
The South Tynedale Railway, offering scenic heritage train rides.
The Nenthead Mines Heritage Centre, showcasing the region's mining history.

Reflections on the South Tyne Trail
The South Tyne Trail is a walk through history and nature, offering a unique blend of industrial heritage and wild beauty. From the imposing Lambley Viaduct to the peaceful moorlands of the Pennines, every step reveals something new. This trail is not just a route it's a story of resilience, transformation, and the enduring connection between people and their landscape.

Whether you're a history enthusiast, a nature lover, or simply seeking solitude, the South Tyne Trail promises an unforgettable journey.

Chapter 7: The Five Pits Trail – Derbyshire

"Unearthing the Industrial Legacy of the Derbyshire Coalfields"

Description of the Route

The Five Pits Trail is a 5.5-mile route in Derbyshire that connects the former mining villages of Grassmoor, near Chesterfield, to Tibshelf. As the name suggests, the trail runs through the sites of five former coal mines Grassmoor, Williamthorpe, Holmewood, Pilsley, and Tibshelf that once dominated the region's landscape.

This accessible, well-maintained path winds through woodlands, wetlands, and meadows, offering glimpses of how nature has reclaimed the scars of industrial activity. Perfect for walkers, cyclists, and horse riders, the trail is a poignant reminder of Derbyshire's coal mining heritage and a celebration of its transformation into a haven for wildlife and recreation.

Historical Background

The Five Pits Trail sits on the remnants of the Derbyshire coalfield, which was a key driver of the Industrial Revolution. For over a century, the mines provided employment for local communities and fuelled the region's economy. However, by the late 20th century, the coal industry had declined, and the mines were closed, leaving behind a landscape of spoil heaps and disused infrastructure.

In the 1980s, the decision was made to transform these industrial sites into public green spaces. Through a combination of reclamation projects and conservation efforts, the Five Pits Trail was born, providing a sustainable legacy for the communities that once relied on coal mining.

Key Historical Moments:
- **Industrial Growth (19th Century):** The Five Pits were established as part of Derbyshire's booming coal mining industry, which expanded rapidly during the Industrial Revolution.

- **Peak Production (1920s):** The pits were at their busiest during the early 20th century, employing hundreds of workers and exporting coal across the UK.

- **Decline of Mining (1950s–1980s):** As coal production decreased and cleaner energy sources gained prominence, the pits gradually closed, with the last one shutting in 1989.

- **Reclamation and Renewal (1990s):** The spoil heaps were landscaped, and the former industrial sites were transformed into the trail we know today.

Closure and Transformation
The closure of the Five Pits marked the end of an era for Derbyshire's coalfields. Once thriving hubs of activity, the mines became silent, leaving behind physical and emotional scars in the communities. The transformation of these sites into a recreational trail was not only a feat of environmental restoration but also a way to honour the miners and their contributions to Britain's industrial history.

Today, the trail's tranquil beauty stands in stark contrast to its industrial past, symbolizing renewal and resilience.

Key Highlights Along the Route

1. Grassmoor Country Park:
The trail begins at Grassmoor Country Park, a former colliery site now transformed into a vibrant green space. With its wetlands and wildflower meadows, the park is a haven for birdwatchers and nature lovers.

2. Williamthorpe Ponds:
Once a coal mining site, this area is now a tranquil oasis featuring fishing ponds and diverse wildlife. The ponds were created as part of the reclamation efforts and are a popular spot for anglers.

3. Holmewood and the Railway Bridge:
As the trail passes through Holmewood, walkers can spot remnants of the old railway bridge that once transported coal from the pits. The surrounding area now features regenerated woodland and open fields.

4. Pilsley Meadows:
This section of the trail offers expansive views of the Derbyshire countryside, with gentle slopes and restored grasslands. The site of the former Pilsley Colliery is marked by interpretive signs detailing the area's history.

5. Tibshelf Ponds:
The trail concludes near Tibshelf, where ponds and woodland provide a peaceful ending to the journey. Tibshelf was home to one of the first recorded railway lines in the world, used to transport coal from the mines.

Walkers' Experience
The Five Pits Trail offers a mix of flat, easy walking paths and slight gradients, making it suitable for all ages and abilities. Benches and picnic areas are scattered along the route, allowing walkers to rest and enjoy the scenery. The reclaimed landscapes create a sense of quiet seclusion, with every section offering a glimpse of how nature has healed over time.

Seasonal Beauty:
- **Spring:** Wildflowers bloom along the trail, and the air is alive with birdsong
- **Summer:** Lush greenery and sunny skies make it the perfect season for family walks.
- **Autumn:** Golden leaves and crisp air enhance the trail's beauty.
- **Winter:** Frost-covered fields and bare trees give the route a stark but peaceful atmosphere.

Stories from the Trail

"Coal and Community"
The Five Pits were more than industrial sites—they were the heart of the communities they served. Stories of camaraderie, resilience, and hard work define the legacy of the miners who worked here. Many local families still recount tales of life in the coalfields, passing on memories of the past.

"The Reclamation Revolution"
The transformation of the coalfield into a trail is a testament to the power of community action and environmental restoration. Local volunteers played a key role in clearing and planting the sites, ensuring that the land was returned to nature.

"The Tibshelf Railway"
Tibshelf holds a unique place in railway history, as one of the earliest industrial railways in the world operated here. Built in the late 18th century, it paved the way for modern transport systems.

Practical Information for Walkers
Length: 5.5 miles (linear).
Starting Point: Grassmoor Country Park; parking and facilities are available.
Difficulty: Easy; suitable for walkers, cyclists, and horse riders.
Best Time to Visit: Spring and autumn for the most vibrant scenery and comfortable weather.

Nearby Attractions:
Hardwick Hall, a stunning Elizabethan manor house managed by the National Trust.
The Chesterfield Canal, perfect for boat trips and additional walks.
Bolsover Castle, a historic landmark with panoramic views of the Derbyshire countryside.

Reflections on the Five Pits Trail
The Five Pits Trail is more than a path—it's a journey through Derbyshire's industrial past and a celebration of its regeneration. Walking the trail offers a unique perspective on how the land has been transformed from coal mines to community spaces. It's a testament to resilience, both of the people who worked the pits and the nature that has reclaimed them.

For anyone seeking a short, accessible walk steeped in history and natural beauty, the Five Pits Trail is a must-visit destination.

Chapter 8: The Tarka Trail – Devon

"From Steam Trains to Scenic Pathways in the Heart of Devon"

Description of the Route

The Tarka Trail is a 32-mile linear route running through North Devon, following the old railway line between Barnstaple and Torrington. It forms part of a larger 180-mile figure-eight recreational trail inspired by Tarka the Otter, the famous novel by Henry Williamson. This section of the Tarka Trail is unique in its focus on the historical Southern Railway line that once served the region.

The trail meanders through a landscape of estuaries, quiet villages, lush green countryside, and rolling hills, offering walkers and cyclists a chance to connect with both nature and the railway's industrial past. The well-maintained path is largely traffic-free, making it suitable for families, cyclists, and walkers of all abilities.

Historical Background

The Tarka Trail's railway roots trace back to the mid-19th century, when the North Devon Railway Company constructed the line to connect Barnstaple with Torrington. Initially built to facilitate trade and industrial transport, the line quickly became an important passenger route, bringing holidaymakers to Devon's scenic coasts.

Over time, the railway became a lifeline for the local clay industry, transporting "ball clay," a high-quality material used in pottery. By the mid-20th century, however, competition from road transport led to the line's decline. Passenger services ceased in 1965 under the Beeching cuts, and freight operations ended in 1984. The transformation of the route into the Tarka Trail began shortly thereafter, with local councils working to preserve its historical significance and natural beauty.

Key Historical Moments:

- **Construction of the Railway (1854):** The North Devon Railway opens, linking the agricultural and industrial towns of Barnstaple, Bideford, and Torrington.

- **Economic Boom (1860s–1920s):** The railway drives the growth of North Devon's industries, including agriculture, wool, and clay production.

- **Tourism Expansion (1930s):** The Southern Railway promotes North Devon as a holiday destination, encouraging tourism along the line.

- **Closure and Decline (1965–1984):** Passenger services end in 1965, and freight operations cease in 1984, leaving the line abandoned.

- **Transformation into the Tarka Trail (1987):** The route is reborn as a multi-use trail, attracting visitors from around the UK and beyond.

Closure and Transformation
The closure of the railway marked the end of an era for North Devon. For many, the trains were more than a means of transport they represented connection, commerce, and community. The abandonment of the tracks left scars on the landscape and in local memories. However, the conversion of the route into the Tarka Trail turned a loss into an opportunity. By restoring the tracked for recreational use, the project preserved the line's legacy while revitalizing the region's appeal to tourists and locals alike.

The trail's design reflects a balance between honouring its railway heritage and embracing the surrounding natural environment. Visitors encounter preserved station buildings, interpretive signs, and stunning views that showcase the area's transformation.

Key Highlights Along the Route
1. Barnstaple:
The trail begins in Barnstaple, the main town of North Devon. The historic Barnstaple Station, though modernized, retains some of its original features. Nearby, the Long Bridge over the River Taw offers a scenic gateway to the trail.

2. Fremington Quay:
Once a bustling freight hub for clay exports, Fremington Quay is now a tranquil stop with a café, a heritage centre, and spectacular views of the Taw Estuary. Interpretive signs tell the story of the quay's industrial past.

3. Instow:
This charming village is a highlight of the trail, with its sandy beach, scenic waterfront, and a nostalgic signal box from the railway's operational days. The estuary here is home to diverse bird species, making it a popular spot for birdwatchers.

4. Bideford:
Known as the "Little White Town" due to its gleaming whitewashed buildings, Bideford is steeped in maritime history. The preserved Bideford Station features a small museum showcasing railway memorabilia. Nearby, the River Torridge adds to the area's charm.

5. Watergate Bridge:
A significant historical structure on the trail, Watergate Bridge spans a quiet section of countryside. The bridge's design is a testament to Victorian engineering, and it provides walkers with a sense of connection to the railway's past.

6. Torrington:
The trail concludes in Torrington, a market town with deep historical roots. Torrington Station has been converted into a café and a visitor centre for the Tarka Trail, offering refreshments and insights into the line's history.

Walkers' Experience

Walking the Tarka Trail is a journey through tranquillity, history, and natural beauty. The flat terrain and wide paths make it accessible to all, while the changing scenery—from estuaries and marshes to meadows and wooded areas—ensures there's always something new to see.

Seasonal Highlights:

- **Spring:** Wildflowers line the trail, and migrating birds return to the estuaries.
- **Summer:** Long, warm days bring vibrant greenery and opportunities for riverside picnics.
- **Autumn:** The trail is awash with golden hues, and the cooler air is perfect for walking.
- **Winter:** Quiet and serene, the trail offers frosty views of the estuaries and countryside.

Stories from the Trail
"The Clay Trains of Fremington Quay"

At its height, Fremington Quay was one of the busiest clay ports in the UK. Trains would arrive daily, laden with ball clay destined for international markets. Workers at the quay developed close ties with the railway staff, and their stories of camaraderie and hard work are still remembered by locals.

"The Royal Visit to Instow"

Legend has it that King Edward VII visited Instow in the early 20th century, arriving by train. The royal connection added prestige to the line and made the village a popular destination for tourists.

"Tarka's Tracks"

Fans of Tarka the Otter will recognize many of the locations mentioned in the novel along the trail. Henry Williamson's vivid descriptions of the Torridge Estuary and the Devon countryside bring the journey to life for those familiar with his work.

Practical Information for Walkers

- Length: 32 miles (linear).
- Starting Point: Barnstaple Station, with parking and public transport links available.
- Difficulty: Easy; suitable for all ages and abilities.
- Best Time to Visit: Late spring to early autumn for mild weather and lush scenery.

Nearby Attractions:

- RHS Rosemoor, a world-renowned garden near Torrington.
- Appledore, a picturesque fishing village with a rich maritime history.
- Braunton Burrows, a UNESCO Biosphere Reserve with extensive sand dunes and wildlife.

Reflections on the Tarka Trail

The Tarka Trail is more than just a walking route; it's a living history lesson wrapped in the natural beauty of North Devon. The repurposed railway line serves as a reminder of the region's industrial and literary heritage, while its tranquil paths offer a chance to slow down and reconnect with the environment.

For those seeking a journey through history, nature, and storytelling, the Tarka Trail is an unmissable adventure.

Chapter 9: The Mawddach Trail – Gwynedd, Wales

"A Scenic Journey Along the Estuary's Edge"

Description of the Route

The Mawddach Trail is a stunning 9.5-mile journey that follows the course of the old Barmouth to Ruabon railway line along the picturesque Mawddach Estuary. Starting in the historic market town of Dolgellau and ending at the seaside town of Barmouth, the trail offers sweeping views of the estuary framed by the dramatic mountains of Snowdonia National Park. This tranquil, flat route is accessible to walkers, cyclists, and horse riders, making it an ideal escape for nature lovers and families alike.

With its rich railway heritage and abundant wildlife, the Mawddach Trail is more than a walk—it's an exploration of the region's industrial past and natural splendour.

Historical Background

The Mawddach Trail occupies the former trackbed of the Barmouth to Ruabon railway, part of the Cambrian Railways network. The line opened in 1865, connecting the coastal towns of Gwynedd to the industrial centers of North Wales and beyond. This railway played a vital role in the transport of slate from the quarries of Blaenau Ffestiniog, as well as wool, agricultural goods, and passengers.

The railway was particularly famous for its scenic route along the estuary, attracting tourists eager to experience the breath taking views of Snowdonia. Despite its popularity, the line fell victim to the Beeching cuts in 1965, closing to passengers and freight alike. In the 1970s, the disused line was repurposed as a recreational trail, preserving its historical significance while offering a new way to enjoy the Mawddach Estuary.

Key Historical Moments:

- **Opening of the Railway (1865):** The Barmouth to Ruabon line was celebrated for its engineering achievements and scenic beauty, providing a lifeline to the local communities.

- **Slate and Industry (19th Century):** The line became essential for transporting slate and wool to markets across the UK.

- **Tourism Boom (1920s–1950s):** The railway attracted tourists to the seaside town of Barmouth and the surrounding areas of Snowdonia.

- **Closure (1965):** The line was closed as part of the Beeching cuts, marking the end of an era.

- **Rebirth as the Mawddach Trail (1970s):** The railway's track bed was transformed into a trail, preserving its history and offering a haven for wildlife and recreation.

Closure and Transformation

The closure of the Barmouth to Ruabon railway had a significant impact on the region, cutting off a vital transport link. However, the decision to convert the disused railway into the Mawddach Trail breathed new life into the area. The trail's flat surface, gentle gradients, and scenic surroundings make it an inviting destination for all abilities, while the surrounding landscapes have become a haven for wildlife.

Conservation efforts have ensured that the estuary's ecosystem thrives, with wetlands, salt marshes, and wooded areas providing habitats for a variety of species.

Key Highlights Along the Route

1. Dolgellau:
The trail begins in Dolgellau, a charming market town with cobbled streets and a rich history. Once a hub for the wool trade, Dolgellau retains its character with independent shops, traditional pubs, and views of Cadair Idris, a prominent peak in Snowdonia.

2. Penmaenpool Toll Bridge:
A short detour from the trail leads to this historic wooden toll bridge, built in 1879. Adjacent to the bridge is the old Penmaenpool Railway Bridge, now demolished but commemorated with plaques and photos. The George III Inn nearby is a popular stop for refreshments.

3. Arthog:
This small village offers access to trails leading into Snowdonia, making it an excellent starting point for hillwalkers. Arthog Bog, a nearby nature reserve, is home to rare plants and birds.

4. Barmouth Viaduct:
The trail ends with a dramatic crossing of the Mawddach Estuary on the iconic Barmouth Viaduct. Built in 1867, this timber and wrought iron structure spans over 700 meters and is still used by trains today. The viaduct offers breath taking views of the estuary and the surrounding mountains.

5. Mawddach Estuary:
Throughout the trail, the estuary itself is a highlight, with its tidal waters creating constantly shifting views. Sandbanks, salt marshes, and mudflats teem with wildlife, making it a favourite spot for birdwatchers.

Walkers' Experience
The Mawddach Trail is a sensory delight, offering panoramic vistas, the sound of lapping water, and the fresh scent of the estuary air. The flat, well-maintained path makes it accessible for walkers of all abilities, and its gentle pace invites reflection and relaxation.

Seasonal Highlights:
- **Spring:** The trail comes alive with wildflowers, and migratory birds return to the estuary.
- **Summer**: Long days and warm weather make this the perfect season for picnics and leisurely walks.
- **Autumn:** Golden hues and the sight of wading birds create a tranquil atmosphere.
- **Winter:** The crisp air and frost-covered landscape offer a serene and introspective experience.

Stories from the Trail
"The Iconic Viaduct"
The construction of the Barmouth Viaduct was a feat of engineering, requiring innovative techniques to span the tidal estuary. Stories of the workers, who braved dangerous conditions to build the viaduct, are still shared in local lore.

"The Last Train"
When the final train ran in 1965, it was met with a mix of celebration and sadness. Locals gathered along the route to wave goodbye, marking the end of an era for the railway and the community it served.

"Natural Resilience"
The estuary is a dynamic ecosystem, home to otters, herons, oystercatchers, and even the occasional seal. Conservationists have worked tirelessly to maintain this balance, ensuring that the trail benefits both humans and wildlife.

Practical Information for Walkers
- Length: 9.5 miles (linear).
- Starting Point: Dolgellau, with parking and amenities available.
- Difficulty: Easy; suitable for all ages and abilities.
- Best Time to Visit: Spring and summer for the most vibrant landscapes.

Nearby Attractions:
- Cadair Idris, a popular hiking destination with panoramic views.
- Barmouth Beach, perfect for relaxing at the trail's end.
- Coed y Brenin Forest Park, offering mountain biking and additional trails.

Reflections on the Mawddach Trail
The Mawddach Trail offers a unique blend of natural beauty, industrial heritage, and tranquility. Walking along the estuary, with the mountains of Snowdonia towering above, it's easy to see why this route has captured the hearts of so many visitors. The trail is a testament to the resilience of both nature and community, transforming an industrial relic into a beloved recreational space.

Whether you're seeking stunning views, historical insights, or a peaceful escape, the Mawddach Trail promises an unforgettable journey

Chapter 10: The Great Western Greenway – County Mayo, Ireland

"A Coastal Adventure Along the Atlantic Edge"

Description of the Route

The Great Western Greenway is a 42-kilometer (26-mile) trail in County Mayo, Ireland, tracing the route of the former Westport to Achill Island railway. Beginning in the charming Georgian town of Westport, the trail passes through Newport and Mulranny before ending in Achill Sound. The Greenway offers an unparalleled journey through Ireland's rugged Atlantic coastline, with its sweeping views of Clew Bay, lush farmland, and dramatic mountains.

As one of Ireland's first major rail-to-trail conversions, the Great Western Greenway has become a flagship project for sustainable tourism. Its combination of natural beauty, cultural history, and recreational opportunities attracts walkers, cyclists, and nature enthusiasts from around the world.

Historical Background
The Westport to Achill Island railway line opened in 1894 as part of the Midland Great Western Railway network. It was constructed to connect the remote communities of County Mayo to the rest of Ireland, facilitating the transport of fish, turf, and agricultural goods. The railway also played a significant role in Irish history, particularly during the Great Famine, when it served as a lifeline for relief efforts.

Despite its importance, the railway struggled to compete with road transport and closed in 1937. For decades, the disused track lay abandoned until its transformation into the Great Western Greenway in 2010. This revitalization project not only preserved the railway's legacy but also brought economic and recreational benefits to the region.

Key Historical Moments:
- **Opening of the Railway (1894):** The Westport to Achill Island line begins operations, serving as a crucial link for remote communities.

- **Economic Impact (1900s):** The railway becomes a key transport route for fish, turf, and other goods, bolstering local industries.

- **Closure (1937):** The rise of road transport leads to the line's decline and eventual closure.

- **Rebirth as the Greenway (2010):** The railway is reborn as a multi-use trail, promoting sustainable tourism and outdoor recreation.

Closure and Transformation
The closure of the railway in 1937 marked the end of an era for County Mayo. The line's abandonment left a void in the region's infrastructure, but decades later, the disused track was recognized for its potential as a recreational trail. With funding from local councils and tourism initiatives, the Great Western Greenway was officially opened in 2010.

Today, the Greenway is celebrated as a shining example of how disused railway lines can be transformed into assets that preserve heritage, protect the environment, and support local economies.

Key Highlights Along the Route
1. Westport:
The trail begins in Westport, a picturesque Georgian town known for its colourful streets and vibrant arts scene. The former station site now features interpretive displays celebrating the railway's history.

2. Newport:
This charming village sits on the shores of Clew Bay, offering stunning views of its islands and tidal waters. The Newport Railway Viaduct, a key feature of the trail, showcases impressive stonework and provides panoramic views of the surrounding landscape.

3. Mulranny:
The trail passes through the coastal village of Mulranny, where golden beaches meet rugged hills. The Mulranny Railway Station has been beautifully restored and integrated into a local hotel, preserving its historical significance.

4. Achill Sound:
The Greenway ends at Achill Sound, the gateway to Achill Island. This area boasts dramatic cliffs, hidden coves, and rich cultural history. Visitors often continue their journey onto Achill Island to explore its stunning landscapes.

5. Clew Bay:
Throughout the trail, Clew Bay provides a stunning backdrop with its countless islands, shimmering waters, and distant views of Croagh Patrick, Ireland's holy mountain.

Walkers' Experience
The Great Western Greenway offers a seamless blend of natural beauty, historical landmarks, and cultural encounters. The trail's gentle gradients and traffic-free paths make it accessible to walkers of all ages and abilities, while its varied scenery ensures an engaging journey from start to finish.

Seasonal Highlights:
- **Spring:** Wildflowers bloom along the trail, and lambs graze in the fields.
- **Summer:** Warm, sunny days showcase Clew Bay at its most vibrant.
- **Autumn:** The countryside glows with golden fields and fiery foliage.
- **Winter:** The trail is quieter, offering solitude and stunning views of frost-covered landscapes.

Stories from the Trail
"The Achill Disaster"
In 1894, just months after the railway's opening, a tragedy struck when 32 people drowned en route to Westport Station to catch a train. These were seasonal workers returning to Scotland for employment, and their story is memorialized near Achill Sound.

"The Famine Connection"
During the Great Famine, the railway played a vital role in transporting food and supplies to the stricken communities of County Mayo. It also carried emigrants from the west of Ireland to ports where they boarded ships bound for America, Australia, and beyond.

"Turf and Trains"
Turf, a key fuel source in rural Ireland, was one of the railway's most significant cargoes. Locals recall the sight of trains loaded with turf, their smoke blending with the mist of the Mayo hills.

Practical Information for Walkers
- Length: 42 kilometers (26 miles) (linear).
- Starting Point: Westport; parking and public transport available.
- Difficulty: Easy to moderate; suitable for walkers, cyclists, and families.
- Best Time to Visit: Late spring to early autumn for the best weather and views.

Nearby Attractions:
- Croagh Patrick: Ireland's holy mountain offers challenging hikes and panoramic views.
- Keem Bay: Located on Achill Island, this secluded beach is often regarded as one of Ireland's most beautiful.
- Westport House: A Georgian-era estate with gardens, woodland trails, and a fascinating history.

Reflections on the Great Western Greenway
The Great Western Greenway is a journey through the heart of Ireland's rugged west, offering walkers the chance to experience its natural beauty, rich history, and vibrant communities. The trail is a testament to the enduring legacy of the Westport to Achill Island railway and its role in shaping the region.

For those seeking adventure, history, or simply a peaceful escape, the Great Western Greenway is an unforgettable experience that encapsulates the spirit of Ireland's Atlantic coast.

Published 2018
Film Volt Group Publications
ISBN
978-1-326-78084-5